Journey
into Oneness

Journey
into Oneness

Paul Goldman

BOOKS

Winchester, UK
Washington, USA

First published by O-Books, 2011
O-Books is an imprint of John Hunt Publishing Ltd., Laurel House, Station Approach,
Alresford, Hants, SO24 9JH, UK
office1@o-books.net
www.o-books.com

For distributor details and how to order please visit the 'Ordering' section on our website.

Text copyright: Paul Goldman 2010

ISBN: 978 1 84694 827 5

A CIP catalogue record for this book is available from the British Library.

Design: Lee Nash

Printed in the UK by CPI Antony Rowe
Printed in the USA by Offset Paperback Mfrs, Inc

We operate a distinctive and ethical publishing philosophy in all
areas of our business, from our global network of authors to
production and worldwide distribution.

CONTENTS

III. The One

For
Sri AmmaBhagavan

I. THE I

A Self In Seven Parts

It has come to this, the time has arrived
for me to share the introductions
amongst the parts of myself.

Some of you have remained strangers,
hiding in you dark trench coats, hats
pulled down to avert your eyes.

Others, like free children have cavorted
and played wild out in the open, not
concerned with what others think.

And some, oh some of you dear parts,
have held steady the lit candles of love-
knowing certain this day would arrive.

Now, the dance has begun, for in the
brilliant golden Kundalini aura, each
of you have stepped bold into the center

of our mutual ring of perception. I laugh
at how each of you was so ready to come
out, to reveal your truth without judgment.

Each of you has served me well, whether
to keep the silent wolves at bay or to let in
the blinding light of love and joy.

We are at last each one introduced, some
for what only seems like the first time;
others old friends who at last can put

down their boxing gloves as there is nothing left to defend. There is only this unceasing love to let in and revel in the glory of bliss forever

more. The new day of my rebirth has arrived, a symphony in seven parts, as my selves have at last merged into One.

At Last A Beautiful Boy

"Close your eyes
Have no fear
The monster's gone
He's on the run and your daddy's here

Beautiful, beautiful, beautiful
Beautiful boy
Beautiful, beautiful, beautiful
Beautiful boy"
- John Lennon

Yes, John, it has taken me many years
to see the truth!

Indeed, now when I look in the mirror
I fear no monsters as I only see the face
of love. The Beloved herself shines

upon me as if affirming I am the
most beautiful, beautiful boy.

I wish you were here, I wish you
were here, beautiful, beautiful John-

as I am at last a beautiful, beautiful
boy. And I need know nothing more
than this, only being beautiful...

For This Morning

I am present,
everything I could
ever ask for,
I already have.

All that I need do
now is recite my
favorite mantra:

thank you, thank you,
thank you…

I am present.

Anything Could Happen

Warning: anything could happen,
and more likely it will. Yet, the sky
has stayed put not budging an inch;

not a single blue swatch of sky has
ever fallen to this day.

Have you ever seen a giant shoe drop
out of thin air dashing all of your
hopes and dreams?

Alright, things have happened and always
will that give staunch concrete evidence
that the very end of the world,

as you know it, has occurred. Yet, on this day,
you awoke, noticed you were still
breathing and could find nothing

in the morning paper's obituaries about
your death. So, still breathing and not
dead, batting a thousand already, barely

out of bed. Anything could happen!

You could fall in love all over again.
The face in the mirror, your face,
could smile back at you quite pleased.

Anything could happen!

Days could begin to go so smoothly
you could forget to look at the clock
and count backwards or forwards.

You could begin to be alive
in this instant like never before.
You never know. Anything could happen!

Whale Song

Two Southern Right whales
sing to me every night in my dreams.
And I know each note as if it were

being played across the rhythmic strings
of my heart. None of the arpeggio scales
are foreign, each sung in striking chords

I have played before spontaneous-
without musical sight or toned talent.

I feel the current move beneath the waters
of my being as my own molecular
structure answers their oceanic call.

I am changed in ways I have yet begun
to realize and know the tides
have only just begun...

as I sink further and further beyond
the boundaries of this place, further
into becoming no more than

a whale song, myself...

Her Beloved Presence

Just last night, She manifested.
When I turned to ask
where She had been,

no one was there.

For a brief moment,
I felt the old feelings
of false fear settle in.

Yet, in the midst of the very next breath,
Her Beloved Presence

was as real in front of
me as you are here tonight.

What is there left to doubt?
What remains but to surrender?
And surrender...

In Each Breath

In each breath,
a song of our life.
Inhale, exhale
and there is the remainder.
We each sing a melody
unique as there are stars
in faraway galaxies.
OUR journey is our own,
not some distant other's
to emulate or mock.
We are here to be
all, the all of the One,
in each breath.
Breathe...breathe...breathe...
and again...

Beneath Silent Waters

I become still,
in the silent waters-
beneath the surface
of my being.

I enter sacred space,
once more- blessed
by the presence of All

that appears before me
when the veil of here
falls away.

Waves Of Bliss
(The Dance)

I have been struck by wave after wave
of bliss until the next wave goes
unnoticed. Just another nudge,

an acknowledgement of wonder.
The question, oh the ever present
question, what to call this bliss

beyond bliss? Words have risen
their hand beneath ocean currents,
now going down for the last count.

Endless waves wash over me. I
know not even what to do
with more of this.

Yet, here I am standing at the water's
edge waiting, daring the rush, the onslaught
of love to leave me breathless

upon the shore.

Waves, ever waves of bliss, be here
with me always. I dance in your
waters until that is the remainder,

only this dance of bliss…

Divine Pit Crew

This endless racing around the speedway
comes to an abrupt halt as I turn
into the pit road.

Not sure if the dizziness I feel is from
the incessant circles or the sight
of this Divine Pit Crew as the Beloved

races mechanical ratchets around each tire
to release and replace, so that I can
quickly resume the race.

I laugh as She assumes the role of different
pit crew members at once, one adding fuel,
monitoring engine maintenance

and yet another inspecting body mechanics
to see if I have lost any new parts due
to the quantum dynamics of centrifugal force.

Once assured that all is at last well again,
She breathes a breath of ecstasy into
my being and whisks me away.

Somehow, the grip on both the wheel
and stick shift lessens as I relax, bank into
the next dogleg and my return

home fresh from the loving care of my
Divine Pit Crew, always safe and sound,
assured of this, this blissful journey...

Give In Again

It seems to pass the test
of faith is to be visited
repeatedly by doubt
up until the very moment
doubt's mask peels away
to reveal only LOVE...

And in that instant,
there is nothing left
to do- except
believe, just believe,

forever...

Moksha

How is it that I have a lifetime,
even many lifetimes seeking that
which has always been before

my own two eyes? Serenity's
relief from this samsara of my
very creation and nothing less.

The answer is as simple as it
is complex. The land of 'if only'
and 'when will' has been so intoxicating,

that at times I could taste no other
nectar as sweet, even though there
is no mendicant as bitter as that

which is self-induced.

Now that I have just begun to peer
into the vast oceans of existence,
consciousness and bliss,

I have begun to see what I myself
had allowed to remain hidden-
locked away in some tower vault

whose walls only appeared impenetrable.

Last night, the Beloved came calling
and she stayed and stayed and stayed
the whole night through.

I can only pray that this was a wondrous
foreshadowing of that which the eons
have borne witness to: my quest,

moksha, the complete and utter
liberation from the unreality
blessed into a final everlasting

as ancient as it is new...

Knowing, At Last Knowing

To be positive is to land
in the river of eternal bliss
such as this moment,
and only this moment,
can deliver. It is to know
that no matter what illusion
sweeps the desert sands
across our own vision,
we are not stranded.

And this ever love we
feel is not a mirage
to vanish in the tranquil
desert night.

No, we do see the Truth
risen above all else
on this horizon of wonder.

We believe to the very
infinite spaces of our
awakening souls

in this love that shimmers
like a thousand diamonds
in our hearts.

To be positive is to affirm
our gratitude for all of these
gifts given, whether seen or
unseen.

So, go and shed light on
all, especially those who
deny such a light of love
has been lit.

Because, we- you and I-
will change the world
in our lifetimes,

until there is nothing left
but loving, only this burning ring
of love around the planet...

Just Around The Corner

I must have misunderstood him when he said
my life was just around the corner; you know
the life of peace, plenty, prosperity and

sheer satisfaction. I gave a closer listen
as he continued explaining that really I already
had everything I needed. This cool cat left original

sin at the barn door!

Seems I was born perfect and completely awake
to the Divine in me and you; except for the process
of forgetting, I might not be seeking the answers

I now seek. Could it be as easy as flipping the
correct switch and flash in an instant, if not
enlightenment, then at least awake to the pure

potential within and around me. Oh and that bit
about me, well that would have to be left behind
or in a manner of speaking, put that 'me' in the passenger

seat and let I AM drive, the one who is without
judgment or fear.

Don't know about you but if my life is just
around the corner, then I am going to hightail
it to get there and meet myself

coming and going...

Search For Life On Earth

I had gone spelunking with miner's hat
into the farthest depths of the Earth,
to search for any nascent signs of life.

I had grappled with grappling hook,
spikes and boots to travail the highest
mountain peaks to no avail.

Even strapped on oxygen tanks, diving
gear, fins and mask to reach the ocean
bottom and still no conclusion.

Where was this life I sought on Earth?
Had it merely vanished?

This search went on and on like this
for years and years. As everything
progressed, everything remained the same.

Weary from the existential exterior search,
one lone day I sat down to think, for a moment.
The most remarkable thing happened.

The life out there I had searched for in earnest,
began to reveal itself in snippets of awareness.
I was amazed.

All those years spent searching without not
within. To meet only the requirement of
sitting still in the silence, nothing more,

nothing less. The search has not ended but at least I know now where to look.

Ding! Ding! Ding!

Have you ever had a moment
of clarity, when at once you
realize the deck you have been
dealt is not stacked, the cards
though not marked are ALL
golden and you just know
that this boat you are sailing
on is not adrift. There is a Master
keeping the rudder right and it
is no wonder this bliss of all
bliss creeps into every sinewy
fiber of your being and you just
have to smile until your face hurts,
you stop for only a second
and keep on smiling...

Soul Groups

We who enter this circle tonight
know at the depth of our being, that
now is not the first time we have met.

The moment my eyes lock on yours,
you and I know that our bare feet
have walked these same lands together

before; traversed the globe on many a sacred
journey- beneath a thousand suns
and a thousand moons.

This feels so familiar because we have
drummed, danced, chanted and sung amongst
our soul group- here with us now-

as sure as the stars that hang in the night
sky this evening yet hung then, long ago.

Yes, I look around and see each one of you,
not much different than the way I remember
you. You may be a man or a woman now,

old or young, this color or religion or another,
yet the essence of you is revealed in the
stellar depth of your eyes-

and they do not lie!

Unmanned

Funny, I keep seeing your bumper sticker:
"Warning in case of rapture, this vehicle
   will be unmanned."

Every time I read those words,
I just shake my head at what you might be
missing, for the rapture is NOW! If I stick
myself in some distant future, then I miss

the astounding wonder right before me.

Yes, the rapture is here right now. Can you not
see? In each breath, in each twinkling star,
yes, and even right there in your own eyes.

We are in the midst of a grand rapture. Taste
each molecular moment of delight as if
it were your first bite of homemade vanilla

ice cream and be reminded you are already
home. The level of bliss is arising
so quickly that each of us may need to

wear our own bumper sticker:
"Warning, this body is unmanned as I
   am in rapture this moment!"

     OR

"Wake up, the rapture is happening now!"

OR

even: "The body has left the building!"

So, my friends let us not be concerned
with sudden unmanned vehicles, but
rather with our own awakening-

to this ongoing rapture right now.

Knowing Eyes

As if we have seen the mark,
splayed on some distant horizon-
we say somehow we have
missed the target.

If instead the Truth is revealed
that we can no more miss
what is ours alone to do
than we can lose our way.

Just look closer and you
will find what you have
been seeking has always
lain right before your own

two startled eyes,
knowing, always knowing.

Something Is About To Happen

There is a moment waiting for you to leap into.
Why delay any longer? Jump up right now!
Go to the window or the door, if you must.
Shout out, I am DELIGHTED to be alive!
Watch what people do. Shocked at first,
then the glee sets in, like watching that
lone dancer and then one by one,
each watcher becomes another
participant in an endless love loop
gracefully wrapping around the world.

So, do not delay, jump up now
and shout out for PURE JOY,
yes, even that, Wild Joy!

II. THE NOT I

Endless Joy

Moments arrive
by a secret entrance.
I look here and I
am in the midst
of a new moment.
I look away and I
am right back
in the midst
of another new
moment.

Endless moments,
endless joy...

Cracked Open

By now our hearts
have cracked open,
like so many holiday walnuts.

We can even try and scoop
each of the shell remnants
and attempt to replace the covering,

yet we know this is futile.

As once opened, our hearts
continue to expand out from
our individual self into the

world at large. What began
as a place where the light rarely
peeked in, now has this streaming

light showering beams both ways,
into us and reflected out
to everyone we meet.

We revel in this being
cracked open, feeling
wave upon wave

of love pulsating through
each beat of our newly
opened heart, ongoing…

A Radiant Love

Have you ever awakened immersed in
a radiant array of love? This place
where all you know is love, this

point of peace that cannot be explained.

Temporary physicality or false appearance
of anything amiss does not rattle or disturb.
The paucity of parsimony disappears

as the brilliant prisms of love
illumine all your eyes alight upon.

Once you have moved your whole being
into this multifaceted mansion of
radiant love,

the reality of what you have set out to do
becomes paramount and you stop
again, for just a moment-

to bask in the enormity of the all of this
love.

As fresh as new fallen snow, the tissue paper
remnants of illusion that had masked this
love realized to now, gently fall to the ground

and you simply are free to be the love that
you are.

Here Now

I am no longer.
You are no more.
No I-nor you,
Only being.
In that, the Truth
is revealed.

Another's Eyes

Two steps in, you turn
to the One on your right
and the One on your left.

In an instant, you realize
they are one and the same;

each one no different from
the other. All stars nesting
in the same universal sky.

Beneath creed, color, religion
and ethnicity, we each speak
a common language of love,

longing and desire for deep
meaningful connection.

Let us not talk softly about this,
but rather to raise our voices
loud in unified praise

at the reckoning at last
of our own divinity revealed
in another's eyes.

Eclectic Electric Moment

So, the morning begins,
if not ecstatic, at least
a glimmer of understanding
that there is so much more
here than meets the eye.

Nuances tingle beneath crisp
awareness of who we are,
who we could be and the grand
potential arising in each of us.

Can you feel it? Can you feel
the juicy essence of yourself
breaking free, rising to the
surface beyond intellect?

We are on the cusp of this
amazement, this realization
of our connection to the One.

We DO sizzle with it all,
for this IS the moment
we have been waiting for
all of our lives.

We have at last arrived,
again. And, we are so
grateful to be alive,
thriving in the glory splendor

of this eclectic electric moment.

From This Improbable Perch

Seriously, he said, I never dreamed of
sitting here tonight or any other one for
that matter, and telling you that I-

amongst all people- have like Elvis
before me- left the building.

No, you do not quite get the impact
yet. The I that I speak of is me, and

this I has come and gone, in this instant.

I am no longer me or I than you are you
or, the I you refer to yourself much like
the I that I was, had always done.

You see, this whole miraculous shift
has occurred as there is now only
we as we-each of us- is merged into

the One. The lines of separation, the
barriers of false perception and so many
more fictitious creations have evaporated.

From this improbable perch all eyes
are joined, hearts entwined in keen
awareness of just how far humanity

has come and how quickly now
that the race has begun, the finish,

the glorious finish line is drawing
ever closer. And at the Divine
moment when all striving ceases

and awareness is everything, we
will each be aligned with every
molecule of love vibrating
and we will see everything, anew...

Who Wants Ice Cream?

In Truth, We are One
Mind, one body,
one soul.

Yet, the lines of
separation remain-
demarcations in the sands
of time.

We, you and I, must
erase these fictional
barriers, break free
to a new unity,

where difference is only
noticed- as flavors
of sweet ice cream.

Alpha Omega

There is a world
of matter, a world
of antimatter, a place
of you and me,
a place where we
do not even exist.
Let the two intersect,
galactic collide into
a space of perfect presence
without end, without beginning.
Which one of us is alpha,
omega? Or are we just?...

Like Sky

I am expansive,
like the sky.
I float in a clear blue

aura of being. No longer
am I concerned with
ending and beginning.

I am expansive
like the sky.

I am air, I am breeze,
I am the essence of blueness.

I am all of this and I am
nothing.

I am expansive
like the sky.

I am.

Ocean Wings

And now we have arrived
in this moment, the one
where memory has us
entranced in an ocean
of gentle waves of emotion.

Each one landing,
as if we had both
wings and a silver surfboard
underneath our steady feet.

Not a drop of fear, only
this steady rhythm of realized
possibility.

Baptized again by our own
reborn faith, walking on
water is not the question

rather the solution to pebbles
that have up until this time,
been strewn about the path

unfolding. No longer as the
tide brings in new wave upon
wave of sanctity, purpose

and a passion to keep on
doing the next right thing-

sailing, ever sailing

on ocean wings...

I Release

I release every single infinitesimal
ion of my being: my thoughts,
my emotions, my desires, and my beliefs,
everything at once.

In this glorious instant, my soul soars
to heights beyond imagining,
as I traverse the farthest reaches of
the Universe. I am nothing, I am

each quantum nano particulate
of matter sailing the electromagnetic
seas at the speed of light.

I release, I release, I release…

Lights On

You and I are called right now
to our sacred purpose. We are here
to shine our own innate light

out to a world which hungers for
love, for a knowing that every
single thing we each seek

shall come to pass. The dreams in
our hearts, each one longing for
a peace everlasting, will come

to this new day of fruition. The news
is good and it is now here. We are
the agents of change. I am the love

you are. We each shining our own
light, see the Divinity sparked in
another's eyes and at once

we have arrived at the precious Truth.

Not one of us is separate from each other.
We, all beings of light and love, are
here now to raise the very vibration

of our tiny fragile planet- to be our
own ordained salvation.

Yes, we know now that turning on our
own light from within, is the way

to at last cleanse this murky environment

of not knowing. We, happily jump into
this new energetic field of light and see
with lights on that there is no turning

back this massive wattage of wonder.

Is Today The Day?

Words etched in Sanskrit
appear at twilight where
my feet touch the ground:

Om Shanti Om.
Om Shanti Om.

Across my path lies
a whispering snake,
I hear amidst her slumber:

Kundalini, kundalini awaken!

A flash of heat arises
within me as the question
is asked, than answered:

Bliss?

Om Shanti Om, Om Shanti Om.

Sacred Voice

How many times have I wished
in the shouting world I could
just return to paying attention?

To hear your Sacred Voice
above the drone of constant
commotion.

Where is this promised solace
of which I have heard?

I seek nothing less than the
reverent silence where all else
stops. Confusion is then cast away

to a deserted island inhabited
by a million stragglers of thoughts
set adrift in my psyche's sea long ago.

I am reminded that invention is only
seeing the same thing different than
before.

Something shifts in the next
breath of realization.

Covered in the dust of my
neglect, the cushion calls,
a beckon back to my home.

I seek to fall into the bottomless

well of silence where nothing
is heard except your Sacred Voice.

No words, no thoughts, only a deep
knowing of your love, grace and
unfathomable acceptance.

Here, I find my center and yours
collide. I enter the Ocean of your
Oneness and I feel complete.
Sacred Voice, it is you I long
to hear and nothing else.

Sow The Seeds of Love

Imagine yourself the gardener of love,
your sack of seeds draped over shoulder
with trowel in hand and garden kneelers

protecting your knees. For you know
this work you are about, does require
time aplenty spent on bended knees

to proffer the prayers of love.

Load up everything you own into the
rustic blue Ford pickup as you hit
the road of your life, certain knowing

that you will be led to where your
seeds can be sown to produce
the most bountiful crop.

A final check in the mirror with the One
you serve, a tweak of your Raffia straw
hat, and then off you go with your fresh

bushel of faith- ready, ever ready,

to sow the seeds of love.

The Flimsy Gauze of Misperception

has fallen away, dust to dust.
Eyes once glazed over from the fog
of a world seen only in duality's

trap, have begun to witness what
the ancients talked about in dreams.

Monotone, monochrome were not
the envisioned saints. Richness
is not lost in a true believer's sight

in seeing beyond the veil of appearances.
To know that what is seen is impermanent
is to hold grace and beauty as majestic

as the Himalayan Plateau in the palm
of your hands.

Only in seeing beyond substance to
a place of peaceful rest, does each
instant of miracle reveal itself.

Of course, nothing has changed,
nothing except- the flimsy gauze
of misperception has fallen away,

dust to dust...

Sprawling Delight

Something happened overnight while
I slept, as the entire scene had changed.

Whole developments of delight
had been constructed in all shapes
and sizes: condos, town homes

and even a few palatial estates
beaming with wonder and mirth
overflowing.

Even the people that populated
these places were different too.
In place of the daily grind frowns

were the most ebullient smiles.

Imagine, if you will, an entire
world sprawling with ECSTATIC
delight...imagine...

The Curtain Pulled Back

Tonight, the house lights were dimmed
as the audience hushed at the moment the stage
curtains were slowly opened.

That is how it seemed, the instant
illusion's veil gave way to a sight
so splendid that I could not be reassured

of its reality. No Gabriel's horns nor
Angelic Choir harkened, but before I
could bask in this revelation too long,

each of the dear things I
had held as certain- one by one
appeared on stage to sing a soliloquy

to prove their own existence.

Some were funny, others were sad.
Yet, in the end, each one vanished dust
to dust to reveal another hidden golden

nugget.

Yes, the curtain pulled back tonight
and everything shimmers at a new
magnitude.

The veil has fallen away
and only the sweet whisper
of Truth remains...

There Is A Spot

in a Universe light years away
where I know I was born. At
last I have found you.

One look at these stellar images
of swirling cosmic matter
and I know that I have found
my way home.

A lifetime spent wondering,
every ounce of my being held back
by the gravitational pull of this lovely

speck of a planet;

and now, I am at once flooded with a new
luminosity. My ears now hear the quasar
pulse of your galactic nucleus.

Your love radiates at a frequency
that my heart has longed to feel
again. All I want to do is free-fall

into your galactic arms, just free-fall
into your loving
galactic arms...ever and ever,

without end...just free-fall into
the purple swirls of your infinite love.

I have come home...

Constant Bliss

Once in a while,
we sit silent.

In these moments,
memory sifts into
the spaces of this still place.

We again remember
everything and wonder
in the midst of the next

breath- if we will forget
again. How could we
in the face of this constant

bliss? How could we?

III. THE ONE

This Big

Heart wide open,
I soar past moons,
suns, stars, even
galaxies to once again
find you,
right in the midst
of where
you have
always
been.

In Our Dreams

In our dreams we travel beyond place
and time to a reality we seem not to know
when awake.

Our task the it would simply seem-
is to awaken, awaken to this land of dreams.

Visualize

Visualize a path
that takes you and only you,
to a secret sacred place
you have only known in your dreams.

Begin to take the first tentative steps
along the well-worn footprints
you now recognize as your own.

Here and there you see signs
left among the thorns, thistles
and flowers. You are sure
this is where you are gathering

together-at last- the parts of yourself
you have to this point not included
in the play of your own life.

It feels so good to let each one
come out and reveal the breadth
and depth of your own being.

For a second, you allow yourself
to drift, to wonder what has taken
you so very long to arrive here

at your very center, the core
essence of your astonishing light.

On bended knees you sing, yes sing
in a voice you have never given credence

to before, sing your praises of gratitude
in amazement at realizing who

you are. No, there is no turning back
from this instant, only a constant
easy stride in grace for each

ecstatic eclipse of moment. You
are finally here and you
are ever grateful to just BE

once again.

Knowing One

We who are One
with each other,
journey from the Source
of Love,

step by step to return
to this same
Source.

Along the way,
at times, we may become distracted
by this or that
and forget for a brief

moment the connection
of one to another.

Realization of this cognitive
distortion shifts us back
to the Truth. We see our
self looking

back from the One
who sits next us,
the Knowing One.

We who are One
with each other...

Smiling For No Reason

How far can we travel
to the unknown and still
remain in the known?

As nothing surrounds us
we become greater than we were
and everything becomes what is,
unfettered with judgment, artifice
or belief in this and that.

A grand settling down into
IS happens and the breath
just goes in and out,
as smile after smile arises...

In Perfection

The mirror of our imperfection
evaporates in wisps of air,
as the Truth of who we are

manifests- now seen through eyes
Divine. All roads offer only
lanes that gently merge in one

direction. The upward spiral's
siren call has been heard and
we do nothing and we do everything.

Transcendence awaits.
And we know there is so
much time for all that is to pass through

us like whispers. We whistle
a tune heard by a new breed,
as the call of Grace sweeps

across the landscape- crisp,
serene and in Divine perfection.

Love You

A sacred voice calls out the words,
"Love you. Love you."

There is no reference to an I as if
there is no person there, no being,
no other, just the One of all.

Love you is a gift of Truth wrapped
in the smallest of packages, just
two simple words.

In this love, I am awash in an ocean
of deep blue bliss. I am a dolphin
leaping across stellar waves.

The salty sea foam rests on my upper lip
as I round the words love you and feel
their essences baptize me. Nothing to

confess or reveal as I know the truth of
my own being is love. All the ancient
beliefs of sin handed down have nothing

to do with this love. Any time I have simply
missed the mark is only a reminder to step
back into the sweet spot of love.

Love you brings me back to I AM, to this
moment of molecular bliss, to a reckoning
of my innate perfection.

Love you. Love you. Love you.
Words of breath. Words of completion.
I AM.

Knowing The Divine Hand

It really does make a difference
knowing the Divine has a hand
in all of this. Yet it goes beyond

this in realizing my own connection
to the Divine, a deeper reckoning
of my own Divinity.

I imagine myself sitting here holding
the hand of the Master, seeking
everything and sensing more than this

pass through skin, to veins, to cells,
to molecules, even beyond quantum
level of either sensation or understanding.

If I were to arise and surely go through
my day with my human hand wrapped
in the loving hand of the Master, what

miracle would be wrought? Or closer
to actuality, I can even now begin to see
a glimmer of *this* reality. Once I let

go and believe in all of this, I am gone,
nobody at home and life is so good.
I want this to last forever...

Our Singular Expression

In a moment
our Truth, that one,
the one we have waited for all
our lives, appears.
Our hearts skip a beat
as we settle into
the sheer amazement
of living, not even
aware that we have
shifted from existence
as our singular expression.

Chance

If there is even a chance
that your devotional chants
will take me to that inner plane

of both Divine potential and
realization, then I am there
diving in with ears and heart

wide open, ready, ever ready...

Om Shree Matre Namaha
I bow to the Mother
Jai Ambe Gauri,
Hail to The Golden Mother
Jaya Jagatambe, Hey Maa Durga!
Victory to Maa Durga, The Mother of The World!

The threads of your ancient chants
weave golden in the opening lotus
of my heart. I feel your words pouring

into the chalice of my vessel and
my cup surely runneth over with love,
pure Divine love. Oh, Holy Mother

you are with me, you are indeed!

What a time, what a moment,
to feel this ecstatic pulse of
grace shifting, colliding, dancing
in me. To know the same energy

is moving through each one is
awe in expression. I go now to dance,
dance, as this IS my eternal chance.

Harken The Call

Hearing the call of love
once more, we are reminded
of all the ancient wisdom;
we turn away from that
which no longer serves us
and walk toward the startling
light, into the revelation
of everything. We remember
this day all over again, falling
deeper, ever deeper into
a Divine Love. What more
bliss can one ask for?
What more?...

Popcorn Oneness

We have arrived at this instant, each one
popping awake like so many kernels
of corn set to burst by the heat of

our own understanding. As if, by each
of us bumping into the bliss of another,
we are startled into this new land of constant

calm. Beware whom you sit with to invoke
the Divine for you may just be in the midst
of another burst of sudden awakening.

Pop! Pop! Pop! Pop! Pop! Pop!

The circle expands in rhythm, in cadence with
our own quickened desire to be alive, to know
doubtless that we are so much more than the

many-feathered illusions we had mistakenly bought
at the traveling carnival that came to town one
fateful summer.

Pop! Pop! Pop! Pop! Pop! Pop! Pop! Pop! Pop!

Feel your heat rise unexpectedly as you burst
open your popcorn heart to let in the ever expanding
light of awakening. A tender joy settles into you

as your smile illumines even darkened rooms and
you become accustomed to this ever present
Pop! Pop! Pop!...

In One Moment

All eyes shifted toward
the patterned sky,
seeking signs of the times

to come. From the outset
none of this made sense,
than wasn't that the point

of being at once awakened.

Through the ancient eyes'
of soul memory, the unseen
began to be recognized.

As the familiar faded to black,
a new reality emerged more
striking than any ever experienced.

You looked at me as differently
as I looked at you, as if we were
both looking at the same One.

In one moment, each person's
persona, slipped away as
one illusory manifestation

after another simply vanished.
The ancestral chants rose above
the din that still persisted beyond

the boundaries of our own sensation-

until nothing was heard beneath
this constant chanting of sacred vows.

In one moment, we are now forever,
in one moment...

Standing On The Edge Of Another Miracle

Tonight, right now, I am standing
on the edge of another miracle
wondering how I was able

to get by- before I believed
beyond what my eyes saw?

Seeing now from the center of
my open heart in each molecular
moment, all the bountiful
abundance that shimmers

in such splendid magnificence
I know there is no turning back.

There is only this breathtaking
feeling of standing on the edge
of another miracle.

This Evening

I dropped into the waiting
lap of my Beloved.

Stars began to fall from the sky
as I settled in for a long winter's
rest. Each breath pulled me
in deeper, nearer, until

silence settled in around me
like a fresh woolen blanket.

My mind went blank as I began
to drift from this space of known
to the vast cosmic ocean

of consciousness. All thought had ceased.

I was simply at rest as I had
embarked on this silent journey
to my home.

This evening I dropped into
the waiting lap of my Beloved
and went home, again.

This, All of This

This, all of this,

by the Divine...

Author Biography

Paul Goldman is an Ecstatic Poet who diligently transcribes the ecstatic words of love that have been available to him [at least] for the past two years.

Paul Goldman produced the CD Wild Joy Released: The Ecstatic Poetry of Paul Goldman with the assistance of friend and extraordinary musician Tom Jacobs. Just a few short months after the CD release, Wild Joy: Ruminations was published in 2010 by River Sanctuary Publishing. The poems in this work were compared quite favorably to Rumi:

> "[Written] with the freshness of an adolescent's first love and with the maturity of wisdom in declaring that "the bringer of joy unbounded brings deep sorrow," these "chanted words connect like a string of rosary beads," to reveal a new human, Homo Luminous. The wild, holy energy within this book can burst forth only from a "man who has lost himself in love," such as Rumi and other seers, whose poetry this volume now joins." - Vern Barnet, *Faith and Beliefs* columnist, The Kansas City Star

Paul is the founder and host of The Gratitude Open Mic Night, a monthly venue to promote poets, musicians and artists. This event is offered at Paul's new Metaphysical shop, Stone Spirit Lodge that he operates with his wife, Dawn.

The stated mission of Stone Spirit Lodge is to Awaken Your Wild Joy.

Find more about Paul Goldman at www.stonespiritlodge.com and at his Facebook page, Wild Joy: The Ecstatic Poetry of Paul Goldman.

BOOKS

O is a symbol of the world, of oneness and unity. In different cultures it also means the "eye," symbolizing knowledge and insight. We aim to publish books that are accessible, constructive and that challenge accepted opinion, both that of academia and the "moral majority."

Our books are available in all good English language bookstores worldwide. If you don't see the book on the shelves ask the bookstore to order it for you, quoting the ISBN number and title. Alternatively you can order online (all major online retail sites carry our titles) or contact the distributor in the relevant country, listed on the copyright page.

See our website www.o-books.net for a full list of over 500 titles, growing by 100 a year.

And tune in to myspiritradio.com for our book review radio show, hosted by June-Elleni Laine, where you can listen to the authors discussing their books.

mySpiritRadio